Gladys
on the Go

Gladys
on the Go

in which she finds her destiny

Photos by Kelly Povo
Words by Phyllis Root & Kelly Povo

CONARI PRESS

We dedicate this book to Mary, who is Gladys at heart and in art...Thank you.

First published in 2004 by Conari Press,
an imprint of Red Wheel/Weiser, LLC
York Beach, ME
With offices at:
368 Congress Street
Boston, MA 02210
www.redwheelweiser.com

ISBN 1-57324-969-6

Typeset in Schmelvetica by Kathleen Wilson Fivel

Printed in China
EVB

11 10 09 08 07 06 05 04
 8 7 6 5 4 3 2 1

Everyone thought
Gladys had
the perfect life.

She had the
whitest laundry,

the brightest cookies,

and her breasts
were the talk
of Sheboygan.

But Gladys knew
something was missing.

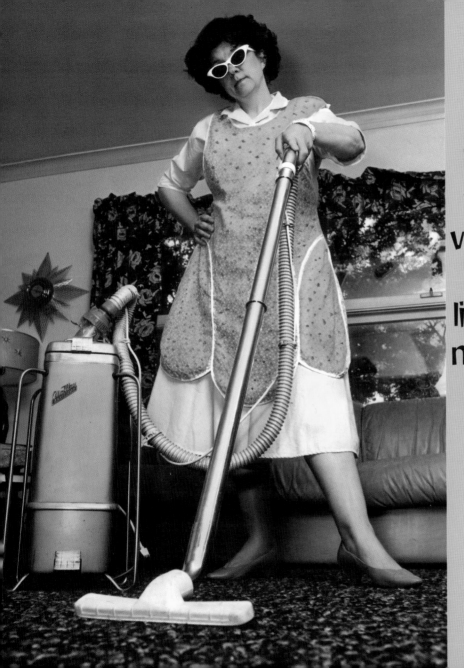

There
was a
vacuum
in her
life that
nothing
could
fill.

Ironing had become a depressing chore,

her
weekly
golf
game
wasn't
up to
par,

and the man in her life
had found a new love.

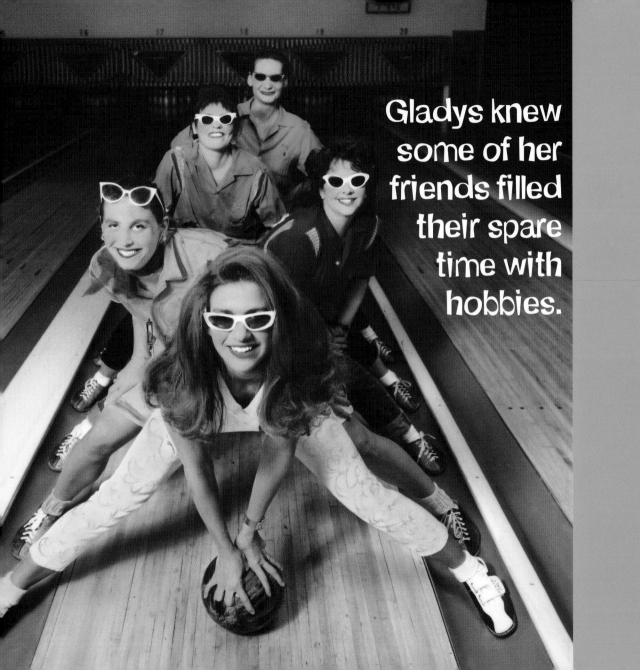

Gladys knew some of her friends filled their spare time with hobbies.

Others threw themselves
into fast cars and faster men.

Still others
found
satisfaction
in discreet
affairs.

Gladys's friends
were full of advice for her.

"There are plenty of fish
in the sea," they said.

But no matter who
they fixed her up with,

he was never Mr. Right.

If life was a game,
she was out at first.

If life was a train, she had been left at the station.

And at the senior prom of life,
no one asked her to dance.

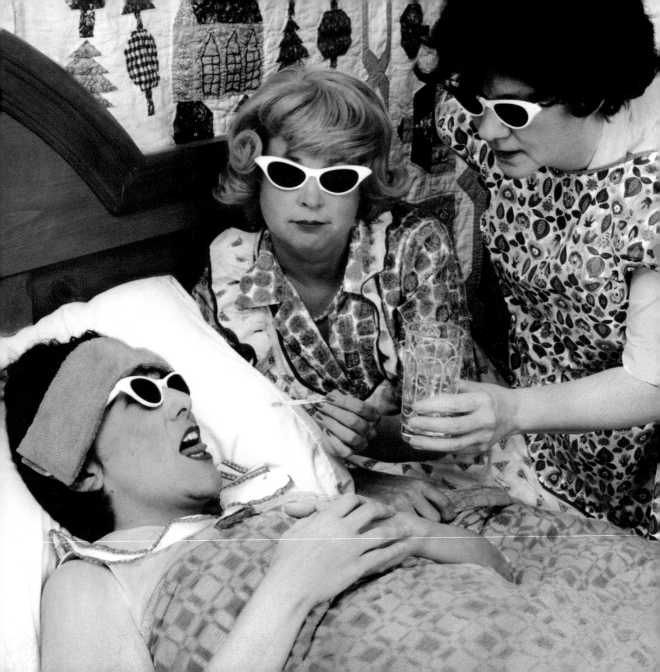

Down and out one day,
Gladys fell asleep.

In a dream, Thelma, the angel of
lost women, appeared to her.

"Listen up, Gladys! If you want passion, adventure, and a purpose in life, you can't just wait for your ship to come in."

"You have to go out and find it!"

Gladys awoke,
her heart
hula hooping
with hope.

She called
all of her friends
and told them,

"I'm off to find
my destiny!"

Traveling light
and always
budget-minded,

Gladys
hit the
road.

She met
sophisticated
women in
New York,

tough-minded
women in Chicago,

Los Angeles women
on the cutting edge,

and women
in Duluth
who would
do anything
for a good time.

Everywhere she looked,
she saw women living their lives
the way that THEY wanted to,

and in a flash Gladys knew,
she could do it too!

Life was a party,
and she WAS invited.

She could dance to her own music,

and sing her own tune.

She could gallop through life,

and steer
her own
course.

Suddenly
life was sweet again.

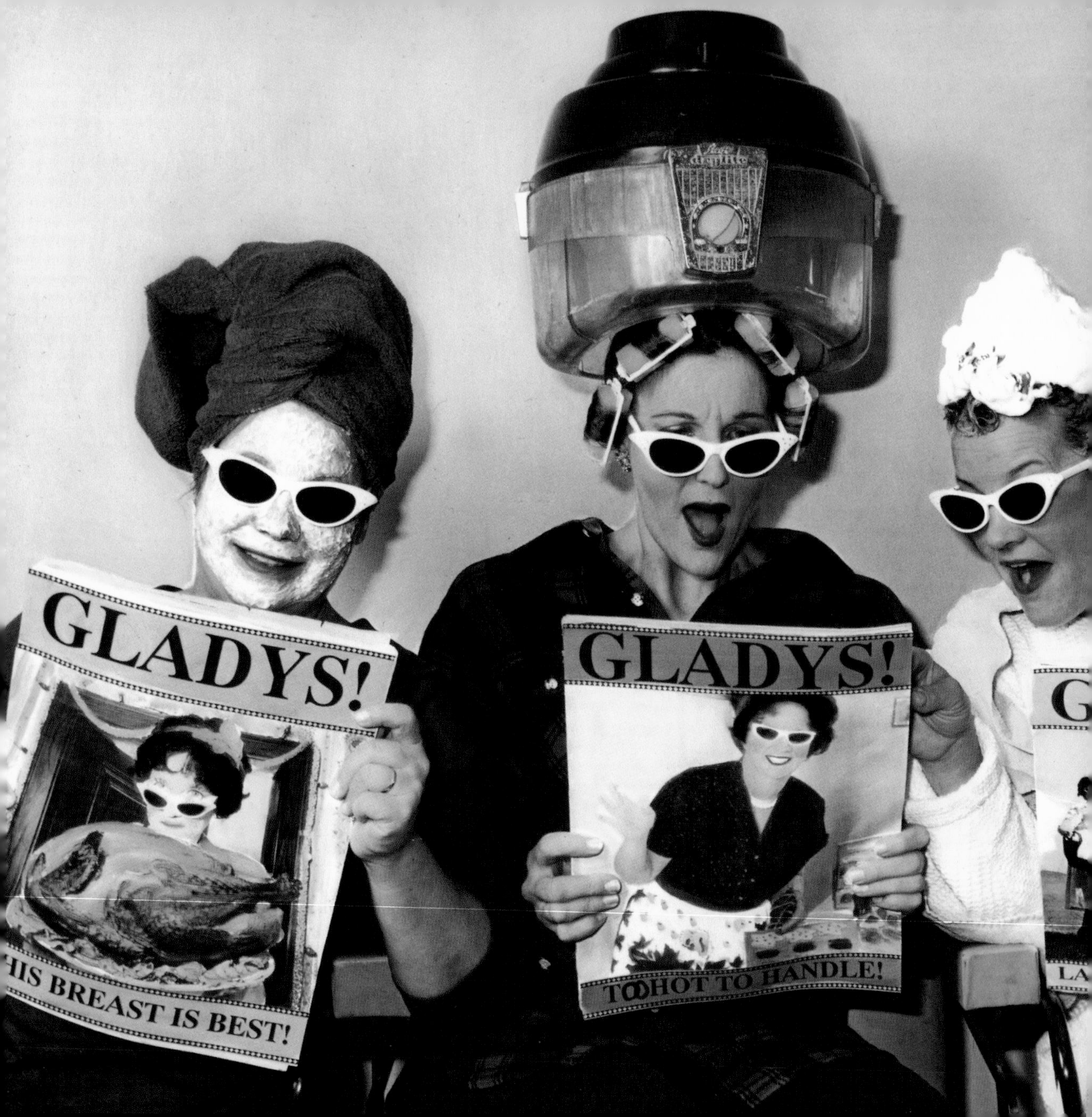
GLADYS!
HIS BREAST IS BEST!
GLADYS!
TOO HOT TO HANDLE!

Perfect or not,
her life was her own.

Gladys was free
and on her way!

What more could
any gal want?

Kelly Povo and Phyllis Root love to be on the go. They have taken many trips on the open road, and though they don't always know which way to go, have always made it safely home, laughing all the way.